Fort Hays

Artist's aerial concept of Fort Hays structures based on a ground plan and photographs of the buildings. This view is from the north and includes all the major buildings at Fort Hays.

Fort Hays, 1889

The parade ground, on the right, has enlisted men's barracks on three sides and officers' row on the fourth. To the left of the officers' quarters is the post hospital, enclosed in a fenced area.

Both Fort Hays and Hays City were named to honor General Alexander Hays (1819–1864). A native of Pennsylvania, Hays was a graduate of the United States Military Academy at West Point in 1844. Among his classmates were U.S. Grant and Winfield Scott Hancock. After service in the Mexican War, 1846–1848, Hays worked as a civil engineer in his home state. When the Civil War began in 1861, he returned to the army. His brilliant career during that conflict made him the most distinguished soldier from Pittsburgh. He was wounded at the second Battle of Bull Run. Because of his record in that engagement he was appointed brigadier general of volunteers and was commissioned lieutenant colonel in the regular army. He was assigned to the command of the Third Brigade of the famous fighting Casey Division, Second Corps, which was charged with the defense of Washington, D.C. He commanded troops at Gettysburg in July 1863 and was one of the heroes of that decisive battle. In early May 1864 the Army of the Potomac, led by General Grant, marched into the Wilderness area and the seven-day Battle of the Wilderness during which ninety thousand men were killed or wounded. Hays, who had been promoted to major general, commanded a division and occupied the key to Grant's position. In the engagement on May 5, the first day of the battle, Hays was fatally shot through the head. His grave in the Allegheny Cemetery at Pittsburgh is marked by a distinctive monument; a monument also stands on the spot where he was killed.

Fort Hays
Keeping Peace on the Plains

by Leo E. Oliva

Kansas State Historical Society
Topeka, Kansas

THE AUTHOR: Dr. Leo E. Oliva is a former university professor of history. He farms with his wife, Bonita, in Rooks County, Kansas, and is the owner of Western Book publishing company. In addition Oliva is a freelance historian whose writing and research has focused on the frontier army and Indians as well as local history. This book originally was published in 1980 as part of a series Oliva prepared on Kansas forts for the Kansas State Historical Society. Similar books on Fort Larned (1982) and Fort Scott (1984) followed. A revised edition of the latter, *Fort Scott: Courage and Conflict on the Border,* was published in 1996. Oliva's other publications include *Soldiers on the Santa Fe Trail* (1967), *Ash Rock and the Stone Church: The History of a Kansas Rural Community* (1983), and *Fort Union and the Frontier Army in the Southwest* (1993).

FRONT COVER: *The Girl I Left Behind,* Fort Hays, Kansas, 1865–1889, by Jerry D. Thomas. Thomas, a nationally acclaimed artist, has made a career of creating wildlife and western art. His original works will appear on the covers of all eight volumes of the Kansas Forts Series. Thomas is a resident of Manhattan, Kansas.

Fort Hays: Keeping Peace on the Plains is the second volume in the Kansas Forts Series published by the Kansas State Historical Society in cooperation with the Kansas Forts Network.

Additional works in the Kansas Forts Series
Fort Scott: Courage and Conflict on the Border

Original title: Fort Hays, Frontier Army Post, 1865–1889
Copyright © 1980 Kansas State Historical Society
Revised Edition 1996

Library of Congress Card Catalog Number 80-82227
ISBN: 0-87726-020-6

Printed by Mennonite Press, Inc., Newton, Kansas

Contents

Foreword

America's western military outposts were important agents in the settlement process. In Kansas, west of Forts Leavenworth and Scott, the establishment of these posts preceded significant white settlement. This of course was bad news for native inhabitants, but it was good news for officials of the territory and later state of Kansas who wanted the region populated by industrious yeoman farmers and their families — the engines of a "progressive" future. The frontier forts of Kansas of the last half of the nineteenth century made this possible: first by bringing people — military and civilian — to central and western Kansas, and then by providing a measure of protection to the routes of travel (stage lines and railroads) and the thousands who came seeking their fortunes or at least a better life on farms and in the towns and villages throughout the Sunflower State.

Leo Oliva's *Fort Hays: Keeping Peace on the Plains* tells the story of one such outpost; a key link in a vast military network designed to facilitate the nation's westward expansion. "The army protected the railroad during and after construction," writes Oliva, "and the railroad was the major factor in the settlement of the region and, thereby, the end of Indian occupation of the land." Although in operation on its present site for more than two decades, Fort Hays was especially active during the early years — the late 1860s and early 1870s. In addition to its major purpose of protecting railroads and settlers, the fort near Hays City served as a military depot, supplying those outposts to the southwest not linked by rail. Once a large complex of forty-five major buildings situated on sixty-five acres with a total reservation of some twelve square miles, Fort Hays is now a historic site administered by the Kansas State Historical Society. The visitor's center exhibits, four historic structures, and additional resources are dedicated to the interpretation of Native American history as well as to frontier military life.

With that goal in mind, the Kansas Forts Network and the Kansas State Historical Society launched the Kansas Forts Series, of which *Fort Hays: Keeping Peace on the Plains* is the second of eight volumes. The series editor and sponsors trust these short histories will contribute to a greater understanding of both the triumph and tragedy of our Kansas and national past.

Virgil W. Dean, Editor
Kansas State Historical Society

1

The Smoky Hill Trail

Fort Hays was one of several military posts established to protect the Smoky Hill Trail, which ran west from Atchison on the Missouri River to Fort Riley in central Kansas and on to Denver. The Smoky Hill Trail was opened in 1859 as the shortest route to the new gold fields in western Kansas Territory, now Colorado. The two major routes, one along the Platte River valley in Nebraska and the other along the Arkansas River in southern Kansas, were approximately eighty or ninety miles longer than the route along the Smoky Hill.

Although a more direct route to the land of golden promises, this new road cut through the heart of Indian hunting lands teeming with buffalo (bison). Indians, including Cheyennes, Arapahos, Sioux, Kiowas, Comanches, and Pawnees resisted this new invasion of their territory. Because of the dangers few gold seekers utilized the Smoky Hill road. But its potential for transportation of people and supplies was promising and the following year, during April and May 1860, the route was surveyed from Atchison to Denver.

William Green Russell, who led this exploratory survey, reported that the trail passed through a land containing adequate supplies of water, wood, grass, and wildlife for food. Later that same year another survey was sponsored by the merchants of Leavenworth to mark a road from their river port to Denver. There was, it should be noted, considerable competition among Missouri River towns for control of trade routes to the West. H.T. Green, leader of the Leavenworth survey, also reported favorably on the route.

1

Butterfield Overland Despatch coach starting out from Atchison for the run to Denver as shown in Harper's Weekly, *January 27, 1866. These fine coaches carried passengers and mail; heavy freight was carried on large wagons.*

Both parties found only one serious drawback to the Smoky Hill road and that was the Indians' desire to keep whites out of the vicinity. It was clear that military protection would be essential to the widespread use of this trail, but that protection was not soon forthcoming because of the outbreak of the Civil War in 1861. Throughout the Civil War Indians resisted those who used this road, and further development awaited the coming of the soldiers.

It was merchant David A. Butterfield who first had the courage to try systematic stagecoach and freight service along the Smoky Hill Trail in 1865. With business connections in St. Louis, Atchison, and Denver, Butterfield founded the Butterfield Overland Despatch (BOD), not to be confused with the more famous Butterfield Overland Mail (headed by John Butterfield) that followed the southern route to California prior to the Civil War. In preparation for his new endeavor, Butterfield sponsored another survey of the trail and built stations. Chief surveyor Lieutenant Julian R. Fitch selected station sites; a construction company headed by Isaac E. Eaton accompanied the party to establish station houses and stables. Fitch selected what became Big Creek Station, a location approximately midway between the first Fort Hays location and the present-day fort site, where he reported that they "made a good rock ford" to cross the stream. This point on the south bank of the creek was designated "a home and cattle station." A home station provided food and a place to rest for passengers and crews; a cattle station was where stock was changed, thus oxen and horses had to be fed and rested there.

The BOD began freight service in June 1865, and stages began running in September the same year. Indian troubles arose almost immediately, and Butterfield sought military protection for his line. General Grenville M. Dodge traveled the route from Denver to Atchison in October 1865 and, impressed with the shortness and practicability of this road, assured Butterfield that the army would give assistance.

There was already one military post on the Smoky Hill Trail. Fort Ellsworth, which became Fort Harker, was founded in August 1864 at the junction of the Smoky Hill Trail and the Fort Riley–Fort Larned Military Road. General Dodge then stationed troops farther west on the Smoky Hill road. Fort Fletcher (which became Fort Hays), Monument Station, and Camp Pond Creek (which became Fort Wallace) were all established in October 1865. The major mission of the troops at these posts was to protect the BOD trains, stations, equipment, employees, and passengers.

Despite the new military posts, Indians played havoc with the BOD because the troops were too few and the distances between posts were too great. Losses of livestock, equipment, and employees to Indian raiders forced the BOD to consider abandoning the route. In addition a railroad was building along the same route and eventually would capture the business of carrying both freight and passengers. The BOD also was losing money, so Butterfield sold out to major competitor Ben Holladay, who operated along the Platte road in March 1866. Holladay did not abandon the Smoky Hill Trail but ran stage service from the "end of track" of the railroad to Denver until, plagued by heavy losses to Indians as was his predecessor, he sold his entire operation to Wells Fargo and Company in November 1866. Wells Fargo sold the Smoky Hill operation on February 1, 1867, to the United States Express Company. This company faced the same difficulties as its predecessors but kept the line in operation for a while. The railroad was receiving more military aid than the stage lines because military leaders saw the railroad as a much more significant development in the West. The Smoky Hill Trail was superseded by the Union Pacific Railway, Eastern Division — known as the Kansas Pacific Railway after 1869 — when that line reached Denver in 1870. With the coming of the railroad, the major mission of Fort Hays troops shifted from protecting an overland trail and the stage lines that operated over it to guarding a railroad in the Smoky Hill valley.

2

The First Fort Fletcher
1865-1866

Fort Fletcher, named for Missouri Governor Thomas C. Fletcher, was established October 11, 1865, near the Smoky Hill Trail crossing of the North Fork of Big Creek, approximately six miles east of Big Creek Station on the BOD. It was situated in a loop on the right bank of Big Creek just above the point where North Fork, also called Victoria Creek, joined the main stream. The camp consisted of tents for men and supplies. By early 1866 the soldiers were living in small log cabins and dugouts that they had constructed.

The founder and first commander of Fort Fletcher was Captain Dewitt C. McMichael, Thirteenth Missouri Cavalry. The initial garrison consisted of two companies of this regiment and one company of the Seventeenth Illinois Cavalry. On November 16 Lieutenant Colonel William Tamblyn and four companies of the First U.S. Volunteer Infantry joined the garrison, and Tamblyn became commanding officer. These infantrymen, known as "galvanized Yankees," were Confederate soldiers captured during the Civil War who were permitted to serve the Union in the West rather than sit in prison.

The primary duty of these troops and others stationed along the trail was, as noted, to protect the BOD stations and coaches from

Stage stations were constructed for protection from the elements and from Indians. Smoky Hill Station on the BOD, approximately one hundred miles west of Fort Hays, was a unique structure. It was built of adobe inside an area dug out of a hill, making it a small fortification. It appeared to be secure from attack and probably was not endangered by the prairie fire sweeping around it as depicted in Harper's Weekly, April 21, 1866.

Indians. In addition they were to protect wagon trains traveling along the route. Fletcher troops spent much of their time away from their post, guarding stage stations and escorting travelers. The soldiers at Fletcher were responsible for protecting the trail from Fossil Creek Station — near present Russell and more than twenty miles to the east — to Monument Station located about ninety miles to the west. Troops located at Monument Station and at Camp Pond Creek were to draw supplies from Fort Fletcher. Supplies for Fletcher were routed from Fort Leavenworth on the Missouri River to Fort Riley, from there to Fort Harker, and finally to Fletcher. Transportation of supplies was a major cost to the government in its efforts to protect the westward movement.

General Dodge, who established this system of protection for the trail, hoped that it would counter Indian resistance and make the route at least as safe as the older, more prominent routes along the Platte and Arkansas Rivers. However there were too few troops with too few supplies to accomplish this, and Indian attacks increased despite the soldiers' efforts. Stage stations were burned, employees were killed, and property was stolen and destroyed. Even the soldiers, when caught in small groups, were victims of Indian resistance. Most stages did make it through because of their troop escorts, but this duty took most of the manpower and left few soldiers to deal with other problems. Since the soldiers could not be everywhere at once, Indians continued their attacks wherever protection was absent.

Another difficulty for the soldiers was that infantrymen, who either rode on the coaches or were hauled in wagons, were unable to deal with mounted opponents. Indian ponies gave the natives a mobility that the soldiers did not possess. Lieutenant Colonel Tamblyn's frequent requests for additional cavalry troops were not filled because the post-Civil War army was being rapidly reduced in size. In addition to inadequate manpower, troops at Fletcher and farther west often did not

This interior view of Smoky Hill Station also appeared in Harper's Weekly, *April 21, 1866. It shows a strong structure that was warm and comfortable.*

receive needed supplies. Soldiers stationed west of Fletcher were forced to come to Fletcher in January 1866 because they had run out of supplies, and many feared that Fletcher would have to be abandoned until the needed food came from Fort Riley.

Indian troubles continued to plague the trail and the BOD in the spring of 1866. Following the sale of the BOD, Fort Fletcher was

Theodore R. Davis was an artist/correspondent for Harper's Weekly *and* Harper's New Monthly Magazine *during and after the Civil War. He visited Fort Fletcher soon after it was established in 1865 and sketched the camp. He later visited Old Fort Hays with the Seventh Cavalry in the spring of 1867 and the new location of Fort Hays during the summer of that same year. His reports and illustrations of the army and Indians on the Plains of western Kansas were major sources of information for eastern readers.*

Missouri Governor Thomas Fletcher was honored for his support to the Union during the Civil War by having the post of Big Creek named for him in 1865.

abandoned on May 5, 1866. The army was shorthanded, funds were unavailable to maintain the post, and Indians temporarily had forced the stageline from the route. This abandonment was not permanent, however, and Fort Fletcher was reestablished in October 1866 to provide protection for travelers, coaches, and especially for the coming railroad.

The site of the first Fort Fletcher is located on private land south of Walker. Some trenches and bake ovens are still visible there, but visitors must secure permission from the owners to see this site.

3

Coming of the Railroad

The advance of the railroad was possibly the most significant event in the opening of the West. That transportation system made possible such developments as the buffalo slaughter, large-scale cattle industry, successful pioneer farming, the end of Indian resistance, the rise of urban oases, and other aspects of settlement of the plains and mountains in the region west of the Missouri River. The army protected the construction and operation of early rail lines, and in return the railroads increased the efficiency and effectiveness of the frontier army.

The soldiers at Fort Hays and other posts along the Smoky Hill Trail were much involved in the development of the Union Pacific Railway, Eastern Division (later the Kansas Pacific Railway). This was the first railroad to build across the state of Kansas. Its route was from the Missouri River along the Kansas River and its tributary, the Smoky Hill River, to Denver. As this land-grant railroad proceeded westward from Junction City, near Fort Riley, it met with increasing Indian resistance. Survey and construction crews were endangered, and the need for military protection was obvious to railroad and army officials. General William T. Sherman, commander of the Military Division of the Missouri, which embraced most of the Central and Northern Plains, believed strongly in the railroad's value to the development of the West and as an aid to the army in its task of removing Indians. Regarding the Kansas Pacific, Sherman called it "the most important element now in progress to facilitate the military interests of our Frontier." Thus he supplied all the military protection for the

Indian raiding in western Kansas increased during 1867, especially after General Winfield Scott Hancock burned the village on Pawnee Fork. Artist Theodore R. Davis portrayed an Indian attack on a stagecoach in his Here They Come *in Harper's Monthly, July 1867.*

This stagecoach with several soldiers aboard as escort is being made ready to depart on a regular run between Hays City and Fort Wallace. After the railroad reached Hays in October 1867 the stages were used only for runs from that point west to Denver. These troops would guard the stage from Hays to Fort Wallace and return from that point to Hays as guard for an eastbound coach. Photograph by Alexander Gardner.

Fort Fletcher soon after its establishment in October 1865 sketched by Theodore R. Davis. A passenger on a BOD coach that passed this site on November 18, Davis recorded: "the fort is so in name alone, as the work is yet to be built. A cotton-wood grove, a sort of oasis in this treeless country, had been selected as a campground, which was not only picturesque but comfortable." Located on the bank of Big Creek and along side the Smoky Hill Trail, the post consisted of tents for troops and supplies. By early 1866 the soldiers had constructed log cabins and dugouts at this site, which was occupied for almost seven months; the remains of some bake ovens built into the bank of the creek may still be seen. After a short abandonment the post was reoccupied at a site nearby. Sketch from Harper's New Monthly Magazine, *1867.*

expanding railroad that his limited budget would provide. To this end Fort Fletcher was reoccupied in the autumn of 1866.

Despite Indian harassment construction of the Kansas Pacific continued rapidly, and the line was in operation to Hays City on Big Creek by October 8, 1867. The following year the line reached Fort Wallace, and it was completed to Denver in 1870. Thus throughout most of its history Fort Hays had the good fortune to be served by the railroad. This made the movement of men and materials economical and easy compared with the

Indian resistance to the railroad took many forms. In this painting Indians are attempting to destroy the Kansas Pacific tracks in May 1867. All damage was discovered by a work crew and repaired before a train arrived. Unable to stop the trains, Indians concentrated on the construction crews in an attempt to halt the advance of the rails.

difficulties of supplying the more remote western military posts. The army protected the railroad during and after construction, and the railroad was the major factor in the settlement of the region, thereby ending Indian occupation of the land. The railroad and the developments it spawned terminated the need for Fort Hays within a few years but not before the most active period in the post's history.

An artist's rendition of an Indian attack on a railroad work party in the spring of 1867. This may be a representation of an event that occurred during the summer of that year when seven workmen were attacked and six were killed. The graves of those six are still maintained by the railroad in a special plot in Victoria.

4

The Second Fort Fletcher and Old Fort Hays 1866–1867

Fort Fletcher, unoccupied since May 5, 1866, was regarrisoned on October 17 the same year by Company C, Third U.S. Infantry, commanded by Lieutenant G.W.H. Stouch. While aid was given to Holladay's coaches using the trail, the major mission, as noted, was protecting the railroad crews. The site of the second Fort Fletcher was several hundred yards northeast of the earlier location, in a loop on the right bank of the North Fork of Big Creek just above its confluence with Big Creek.

Soon after its reoccupation the fort's name was changed. Following the Civil War many posts were renamed to honor Union officers who died in battle. By order from department headquarters at Fort Leavenworth, dated November 17, 1866, Fort Fletcher became Fort Hays to honor General Alexander Hays from Pennsylvania who was killed at the Battle of the Wilderness on May 5, 1864.

Since it appeared that this post was to be a permanent installation the troops stationed there began to construct quarters so they could move out of the tents. This proved to be a difficult task because they were forced to rely on construction materials that were readily available

Despite Indian attempts to stop the Kansas Pacific, the track inched westward across the state. Hays City had rail service beginning October 8, 1867, and the line pushed on before winter stopped construction for the year. In this photo track is being laid approximately twelve miles west of Hays City, October 19, 1867. Photograph by Alexander Gardner.

Cheyenne warriors attacking a construction crew in August 1867. Illustration from Harper's Weekly, *September 7, 1867.*

in the region. Quarters were completed, however, and Captain Albert Barnitz, Seventh U.S. Cavalry, described the post as he saw it on April 20, 1867, soon after his arrival there: "This post is beautifully situated, in a pleasant valley on Big Creek, a well timbered stream of good water — but the post is not equal to Riley or Harker so far as the appearance goes. The buildings are mostly small, one story high and built of logs — except two or three of stone." Actually the post was not so well situated as a flood later demonstrated.

The troops at Fort Hays continued to aid the railroad crews, but the post's location proved to be unsatisfactory for two reasons: the railroad was following a route to the north of the old trail and the fort, and the post was located in a floodplain that could be destructive.

General Winfield Scott Hancock, commanding the Department of the Missouri, made the decision to move the post nearer the railroad while visiting there in early May 1867. He found "no permanent buildings" at the post and stated that troops were housed in log and adobe huts. He determined that the post could better serve the railroad (obviously the post also would be better served by the railroad) if it were moved to a site near where the railroad crossed Big Creek (north of the present site of Fort Hays).

Before this move was accomplished, the second difficulty with the Old Fort Hays site added urgency to the relocation. Heavy rains to the northwest on June 7 sent a flood through the post before dawn the next

General Winfield Scott Hancock, a classmate with Alexander Hays at West Point, had compiled a brilliant Civil War record and was department commander of the region including Fort Hays in 1867. It was Hancock who made the decision to relocate the fort. During an unsuccessful expedition against the Indians, Hancock's actions increased Indian hostility in the region, and he was replaced later in the year by General Philip H. Sheridan. Hancock was the Democratic candidate for president in 1880 and was defeated by James A. Garfield.

day. At least seven soldiers and two civilians drowned and much property was destroyed. Selecting a new location soon followed under the direction of Major Alfred Gibbs, Seventh Cavalry. The present Fort Hays site was officially occupied June 23, 1867.

Activities at Old Fort Hays during 1866 and 1867 did little to quell Indian troubles. Before the end of the year, the post garrison was increased to more than two hundred officers and men constituting troops of the newly organized Seventh Cavalry as well as Third Infantry. Most were involved in maintaining supply lines and protecting stage and rail employees. Small groups of noncommissioned officers and men were rotated on a three-week schedule between the stage stations and railroad work camps in the region. As it turned out little Indian activity occurred during the winter months. The Indians spent their time in winter camps and seldom ventured out to raid. The soldiers, in addition to trying to keep warm, spent much time drilling. Most were recent recruits who

This view of Old Fort Hays was taken in 1867 after the garrison had moved to its new and present location following the destructive flood of June 8. Quarters consisted of log and stone huts around three sides of a parade ground. Note the flagpole, which was made by fastening two poles together.

were expected to be called upon to fight in large numbers during the coming spring and summer of 1867.

In anticipation of this expanded Indian warfare, General Hancock led an expedition onto the Plains in the spring of 1867 to deal with the problem. With a force of fifteen hundred troops, including George A. Custer and the Seventh Cavalry, Hancock led his command from Fort Riley to Forts Harker, Zarah, and Larned. After meeting with Indian leaders at Larned, Hancock led his command to a Cheyenne and Sioux encampment on Pawnee Fork. The Indians were fearful of the troops and abandoned their camp. Custer and the Seventh Cavalry were sent in pursuit on a chase that led them to Fort Hays. On the way the troops saw the results of Indian attacks on stage stations; when this information was sent to Hancock he destroyed the Indian encampment he held. Indian raids increased dramatically during the remainder of the spring and summer of 1867, fulfilling the predictions of a major Indian uprising. Hancock kept Custer in the field to counter the hostiles.

21

Henry M. Stanley, correspondent for an eastern newspaper, accompanied General Hancock during the expedition of 1867 and was a visitor at Fort Hays in early May of that year. Stanley's reports gave eastern readers a first-hand account of the army and Indians, and he was not always complimentary to the military. He described one frontier fort near Fort Hays as appearing like "a giant wart on the plains." In 1869 the New York Herald *sent Stanley to Africa to find David Livingstone. He achieved lasting fame when he found Livingstone in 1871. Sketch from* Harper's Weekly, July 27, 1872.

When Custer arrived at Fort Hays he expected to acquire needed supplies to continue his Indian pursuit, but there was no forage for his animals. It was more than a month before Custer was back in the field, and during that time his wife, Elizabeth, joined him in camp near the fort. Although Custer and the Seventh Cavalry had departed from Fort Hays to seek out Indians, Elizabeth Custer was still encamped there when the flood struck in early June. It was a perilous experience and she went back to Fort Riley soon thereafter.

Major Alfred Gibbs, Seventh Cavalry, was commanding officer of Fort Hays in June 1867. He selected the site of the new post and directed the move to the present location. He was an important officer in the newly organized Seventh Cavalry, for he was a strict disciplinarian and he created the famous regimental band. He had graduated from West Point in 1846 and served in the Mexican War, Indian campaigns in the West, and the Civil War. He was wounded by an Apache lance in 1857 and remained in poor health. Unable to continue in the field with his regiment in 1868, he died at Fort Leavenworth on December 25 of that year. His position with the regiment was filled by Marcus A. Reno.

Custer led his command through portions of northwest Kansas, southwest Nebraska, and northeast Colorado Territory but was unable to find the hostile Indians. The experience was frustrating for Custer and his command. One of the officers, Captain Barnitz, explained the inability of the few troops to deal effectively with an enemy that another officer described as "being everywhere and yet nowhere." Barnitz proclaimed:

George A. Custer and his wife, Elizabeth, were encamped near Fort Hays on several occasions. This 1865 photo shows Mrs. Custer's beauty, an asset that benefited both of them in military and civilian life.

We will fool away the Summer here, without adequate force to accomplish anything, and next Summer we will repeat the experience of this! It needs not less than 40,000 men to make a speedy end of this Indian business, and we haven't a fourth of this number, and our troops are scattered in parties too small to accomplish anything through an area of about 10,000 square miles! By actual statistics 9,700 Indians, of various tribes are known to be on the war path, and others are wavering, or supposed to be leagued with our enemies. Well, a different policy will have to be instituted in the management of Indian affairs, or I fear that by next summer there will be few officers or men left of the regular forces now here. The officers, many of them will resign, and the men will avail themselves of the only opportunity that will be afforded them for getting home, as soon as they arrive once more in the vicinity of the settlements! This is truly a bad state of things, and quite unnecessary I think. It is a "penny wise and pounds foolish" policy, which will produce such results.

The observation was correct in most details, but a parsimonious Congress would not provide the funds needed to handle the situation.

Custer, frustrated by the Indians and longing to see his wife, abandoned his command at Fort Wallace in western Kansas in July and made a forced march and ride to Fort Riley. On that trip he passed the new Fort Hays but did not tarry there. At Fort Riley he was arrested and later court-martialed. He was suspended from service for one year without pay but was back in command and fighting Indians the next year.

5

Building Fort Hays

The major task at the post, following the selection of the permanent location, was the construction of necessary buildings to house men, animals, and supplies. Fort Hays, like the other Plains forts, was not a true fortification but appeared to be more like a frontier settlement. There was no wall around the post, and the only defensive structure was a blockhouse. An extensive bastion was considered unnecessary for little fear existed that Indians would attack a well-armed contingent of troops. The post was designed as a base for supplies and troops who could be dispatched into the field to protect vulnerable people and places when Indian resistance appeared. The buildings, arranged by military plan with housing around the parade ground and supporting structures grouped nearby, were constructed by the troops with the assistance of civilian employees. Although most frontier military posts were designed for temporary service and hastily constructed, the buildings at Fort Hays were considered to be clean and comfortable by the soldiers stationed there.

For several months after the move to the new site, the troops lived in tents a few hundred yards from the post to avoid interfering with construction. Construction took much more time than planned because of several problems.

Soldiers were detailed to work on the buildings and civilian employees were hired to help. Because other military activities competed with construction for manpower, an adequate labor supply was lacking. Often

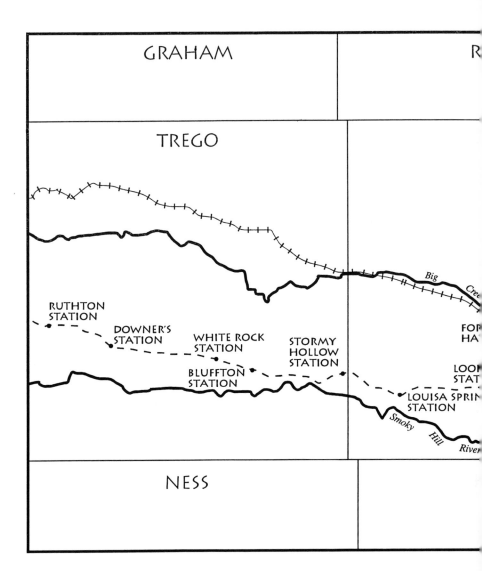

GRAHAM

R

TREGO

RUTHTON
STATION

DOWNER'S
STATION

WHITE ROCK
STATION

STORMY
HOLLOW
STATION

BLUFFTON
STATION

Big

Cre

FOR
HA

LOO
STAT

LOUISA SPRIN
STATION

Smoky

Hill

River

NESS

*Fort Hays was one of several military posts established first to protect the
Smoky Hill Trail and later to guard the Kansas Pacific Railway in the Smoky
Hill valley. The map includes Butterfield Overland Despatch stations on the
trail and the sites of Old Fort Fletcher, Old Fort Hays, and Fort Hays.*

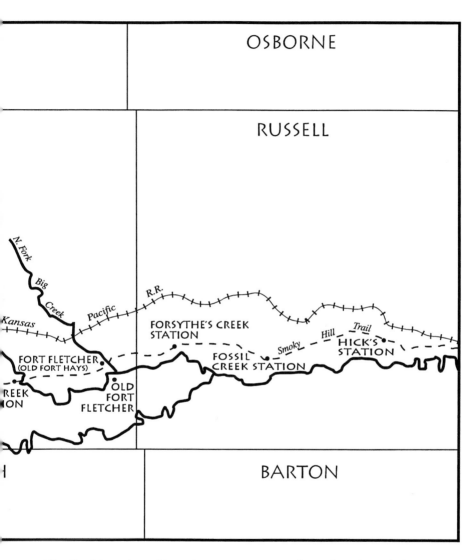

The final location of Fort Hays was nearer the railroad, and the permanent post built there provided security for the settlement of the western Kansas Plains until November 1889, when it was no longer needed as a military post.

the workers, military and civilian, did not possess the requisite carpentry and masonry skills. All building materials except for native stone had to be transported to the post. Lumber, hardware, doors and windows, plaster, and other items had to be shipped from the East at great expense. Once the railroad reached Hays, however, the problem of building material was easier to handle.

Construction of the barracks was desired before winter, and the haste with which they were thrown up created new problems. Most buildings had to be altered and repaired to keep them habitable. Nevertheless, a large complement of buildings eventually graced the Fort Hays site, and the quarters later were described as comfortable. Even while construction was under way, Captain Barnitz declared that "Fort Hayes is, I think, by far the cleanest, and loveliest post that I have ever seen."

The post had four frame soldiers' barracks, each designed to accommodate one company of one hundred men, four frame married soldiers' quarters (sometimes referred to as laundresses' quarters), each containing rooms for four couples, and ten frame officers' quarters. The quartermaster stores were housed in three long frame structures built parallel and connected by roofing over the spaces between, and the commissary storehouse was one long frame structure. The original frame guardhouse was replaced by a stone guardhouse in 1872. The only other stone structures were the blockhouse, which was one of the first buildings erected at the post, and a stone bake house built in 1877.

This 1869 photo of Fort Hays includes most of the buildings erected on the post. This view is from the east and depicts (left to right) the post sutler's store (two story), laundresses' quarters, blockhouse, hospital complex, officers' row, quartermaster warehouses, commissary warehouse, enlisted men's barracks (partially hidden), corrals, and stables.

Colonel (Brevet Major General) Andrew J. Smith was Custer's immediate superior officer. Smith commanded the Seventh Cavalry from its organization until 1869 and was the commander of the military district in which Fort Hays was located. He never took command of the Seventh Cavalry in the field, leaving that to Custer. Smith was at Old Fort Hays in June 1867 when the post was flooded, and five of his orderlies drowned in that disaster. It was Smith who ordered Custer's arrest at Fort Riley following Custer's unauthorized visit to his wife there, and it was Smith who preferred charges against Custer that led to the court-martial conviction. Smith resigned his commission in 1869, and Samuel D. Sturgis replaced him as colonel of the Seventh Cavalry.

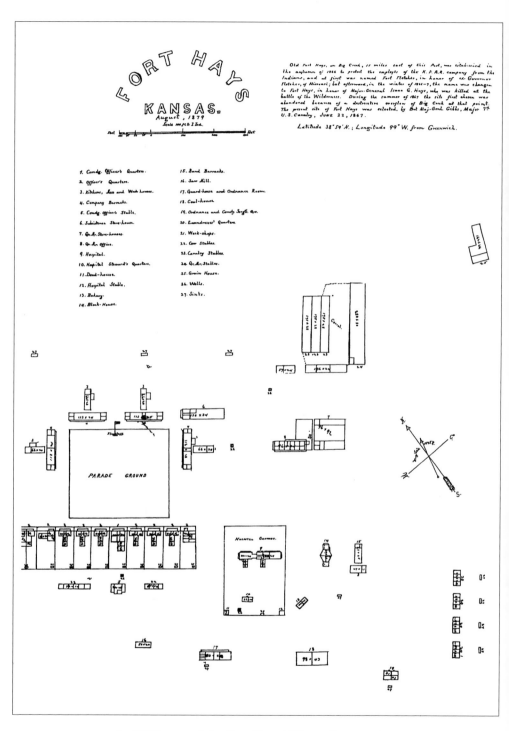

An 1879 map of the Fort Hays Military Reservation.

This view of Fort Hays from the south was taken in December 1873. The stone guardhouse, erected in 1872, is prominent in the left front of the photograph.

The hospital complex was prefabricated in St. Louis, shipped to Fort Hays, and erected in November 1867. Two main buildings were connected by a passageway; one contained a large ward, the other a small ward, a post surgeon's office, and a dispensary. A kitchen and dining room were attached to the rear of the main ward. Later a surgeon's home and a dead house were added. The hospital had no bathrooms and little storage space.

Other buildings included a bakery, stables, workshops, a grain house, and an ice house. Over the years buildings were altered, removed, or replaced, but the post's appearance never significantly changed after major construction was completed in 1870.

A military reservation around Fort Hays was surveyed in August 1867. It comprised some seventy-five thousand acres located south of the railroad. The area was closed to civilian settlers, thus preserving the wood, water, grass, and reservation soil for military use.

Cheyenne Indians were one of the major groups opposing the railroad and the army in western Kansas. Above is a Cheyenne camp with its mobile homes (tipis) and drying racks. Below are three Cheyenne leaders, (left to right) White Antelope, Man on a Cloud, and Roman Nose.

6

Frontier Defense

Fort Hays was established to protect the region from Indians who objected to the white invasion of their hunting grounds, and relations with Indians occupied much of the garrison's time during the post's early years. No major Indian fight occurred in the immediate vicinity, however, and Fort Hays was never attacked by Indians. The Fort Hays troops did help protect the lines of transportation and the settlements that grew up along them, and they assisted with the removal of Plains tribes from western Kansas.

Major Gibbs, Seventh Cavalry, oversaw the move of Fort Hays to a new and better location, but he was unable to deal with Indians troubling the railroad crews. Even though the new fort was nearer the railroad, the garrison lacked sufficient manpower. Gibbs requested more troops and received some companies of the Thirty-eighth Infantry and Tenth Cavalry, both regiments comprised of black soldiers with white officers. In addition, the Eighteenth Kansas Cavalry was organized during the summer of 1867 and served until November that same year. The increase in troops and their proper deployment resulted in a reduction of Indian attacks along the railroad during July, but August saw Indian activity revived on a larger scale. The continuous movement of rails westward into the heart of good buffalo country probably inspired this frenzied opposition. Troops from Fort Hays encountered some of the war parties.

Captain George Armes and thirty-four men of the Tenth Cavalry met a large force, estimated at four hundred to five hundred warriors, of the

Lieutenant Colonel Custer led his troops through a snowstorm to attack the Cheyenne village on the Washita River on November 27, 1868. The supplies for his expedition came to Fort Hays by rail and were sent on in wagon trains. This sketch of his march appeared in Harper's Weekly.

These Indian prisoners on the march to Fort Hays in the winter of 1868–1869 were captured at the Washita battle on November 27, 1868, and released at Fort Hays on June 13, 1869.

Major George A. Forsyth, Ninth Cavalry, was selected by General Sheridan to organize and lead a band of fifty frontier scouts in the summer of 1868. This band often is known as Forsyth's Scouts. Lieutenant Frederick H. Beecher, Third Infantry, was appointed second in command, and an army surgeon, John H. Mooers, was assigned to the scouts. These three officers and fifty civilian scouts were to find and punish hostile bands of warriors. The scouts were recruited at Forts Harker and Hays, outfitted at

Fort Hays, and ordered to Fort Wallace. On September 10, 1868, they were sent in pursuit of Indians who had attacked a wagon train near Fort Wallace. They lost the trail and were attacked by Indians on September 17 on the Arikaree Fork of the Republican River. The scouts took refuge on a small island, which became known as Beecher's Island because Lieutenant Beecher was killed there, but an overwhelming force of Indians charged them time and time again. The scouts lost their horses, food, and medical supplies, but they dug in and were able to avoid annihilation because of their superior firepower (repeating rifles). Within a short time, however, twenty-two men had been shot, including Forsyth, Beecher, and Mooers; the latter two and four scouts died. Forsyth received three wounds and nearly died. Although the Indians moved on after the third day, the scouts were stranded until September 25 when they were rescued by Lieutenant Colonel Louis H. Carpenter and seventy troopers of the Tenth Cavalry and seventeen army scouts. The failure of the expedition led to the abandonment of Forsyth's Scouts. Forsyth recovered from his wounds and retired a lieutenant colonel of the Fourth Cavalry in 1890. He wrote two books, both published in 1900: The Story of the Soldier and Thrilling Days of Army Life. He died in 1915.

The closest association Fort Hays had with Indians was as a prison for the Cheyenne captives taken at the Washita battle. This special pen was constructed along side and to one end of the frame guardhouse and had an observation walk for guards. Many visitors came to the prison to have a close look at the "fierce" Cheyennes, but they found mostly women and children. Despite efforts to make the confinement as comfortable as possible, Indians and guards were suspicious of each other. A misunderstanding resulted in a fight in which two of the three men prisoners, possibly one of the women prisoners, and the sergeant of the guard were killed. The Indians were released and returned to their people in Indian Territory in the late spring of 1869.

Cheyennes and Arapahos near the Saline River north of Hays and fought for approximately six hours, during which time the troops retreated to Fort Hays without heavy losses despite the overwhelming odds. This fierce battle was waged within a few miles of the post. The troops had some men wounded, including Captain Armes, and others suffered from another enemy that faced the soldiers that summer — Asiatic cholera. The 1867 cholera epidemic claimed more victims than did Indians, and that dreaded disease brought heavy losses to the garrison and civilian workers at Fort Hays as well as to many other Kansas forts and towns.

Captain Armes and his men were sent to protect a railroad construction camp located approximately ten miles east of Fort Hays on August 1, 1867. That same day six of a seven-man work party were killed by Indians while working apart from the main crew on the tracks west of

The cavalry stables at Fort Hays were constructed of logs standing upright. Horses were grazed near the post, and they were brought into the stables twice a day where they were cared for by the cavalryman to whom they were assigned. They received a ration of grain year-around and hay in the winter months.

the camp. Sometime the same day a party of Indians stole thirty horses from the Big Creek Station of the stage company. Armes and his troopers followed the Indian trail until nightfall and returned to the construction camp. Seeing a need for a larger force, Armes sent six of his men back to Fort Hays with orders to bring thirty soldiers and an artillery piece back the next morning. Before the reinforcements arrived on August 2 Armes left the camp with thirty-four troopers to attempt to overtake the Indians. He had to leave four men in camp with cholera. It was this small party that was attacked near the Saline River and driven back to Fort Hays. The Indians gave up the fight when the soldiers were near the post. The railroad workers at the camp east of Hays deserted to seek protection elsewhere.

The increased Indian activity in August caused many railroad workers to the west of Fort Hays to leave their camps and come to the post for protection. There, with nothing to do, they began to drink at the whiskey ranches around the fort and became, in the words of post commander Captain Henry C. Corbin, Thirty-eighth Infantry, a "demoralized mob." Troops escorted the workers back to their camps, but messengers visited the camps telling wild tales of Indians and urging them to return

The limestone blockhouse was the only defensive structure at Fort Hays. Originally constructed with rifle slits in the walls, it would serve as a refuge in case of attack. The fort was never attacked, however, and this structure served as the office for the commanding officer, quarters and office for the post adjutant, and contained the library that provided books for officers and enlisted men. Many of the books were military histories and biographies of military leaders, but the collection also included popular fiction and literary classics.

to the fort. They did, and the problems were repeated. It was discovered that the whiskey merchants were sending the warnings. Captain Corbin had the troops confiscate the liquor of unlicensed merchants around the post and sent more troops to escort the workers back to their camps. This time they stayed on the job.

On August 5 Captain Armes led a party of his troops from Fort Hays to a construction camp to the west, hoping to encounter a war party of Indians believed to be in that area. No Indians were found, but Armes claimed that the presence of his patrol along the railroad showed the construction crews that the army was protecting them and encouraged them to stay on the job. On August 8, however, an Indian attack west of Hays caused more workers to come back to the fort. Captain Corbin sent an escort of troops with the workers to return to the camp, but the workers returned to Fort Hays a few hours after the troops arrived back there. More troops were stationed along the railroad, but the situation was desperate.

When Captain Armes — at a camp thirty-five miles west of Hays in mid-August — asked for volunteers to ride to Fort Hays for reinforcements, no one volunteered. Armes took an orderly and made the trip himself, returning with additional men to protect the camp.

Captain Armes led more troops from Fort Hays later in August to find and attempt to destroy an Indian village believed to be located northwest of the post. Indians were engaged near Prairie Dog Creek in northern Kansas, and a lengthy and indecisive battle followed. Armes reported his losses as three killed, twenty-eight wounded, and forty horses lost. Indian losses were unknown. The Indian encampment apparently broke up following this battle, but Indian attacks on railroad workers continued through September.

A peace council was held at Medicine Lodge Creek in southern Kansas in October 1867. There many of the Plains tribes agreed to remove to reservations in Indian Territory (present-day Oklahoma) and give up all claims to lands north of the Arkansas River in exchange for annuities and promises of aid and hunting rights south of the Arkansas. Like Hancock's expedition, however, this too failed to bring peace to the

Fort Hays had two guardhouses. The original frame building, not shown in this photo, was fifty by twenty feet. Because it was inadequate, this larger (eighty by twenty feet) stone guardhouse was built in 1872. This guardhouse has been restored and is a part of Fort Hays State Historic Site.

Captain George A. Armes, Tenth Cavalry, led his troops in two engagements against Indians and suffered a hip wound. His autobiography, Ups and Downs of an Army Officer (1900) reveals an interesting character who was often in trouble. By his own count he was court-martialed nine times. Armes was one of the officers at Fort Hays who invested in the development of Hays City. He raised four hundred dollars to help Joseph Clarke establish the first newspaper in Hays, the Hays City Railway Advance, in November 1867. He also purchased a lot in Hays City where he constructed a building. He was involved in collecting funds that supposedly were to be used to construct a church but instead helped build a dance hall.

Plains. The federal government was slow in carrying out the terms of the treaty, and the Indians concluded that the treaty would not be enforced, so they returned to western Kansas in the spring of 1868 to hunt buffalo and began raiding.

Because of its rail connection, Fort Hays was selected by General Philip H. Sheridan, who had replaced Hancock as commander of the department, as his field headquarters in 1868 while he planned a long-distance, three-pronged attack against winter camps in western Indian Territory. For the same reason, the fort served as the base for Major George A. Forsyth's fifty civilian scouts, raised by Sheridan in 1868 as an experiment to see if frontier scouts could deal effectively with the mobile enemy that often eluded military details. These scouts were pinned down

John E. Yard was a popular officer and commanded Fort Hays for a short time in 1868 while he was a major in the Tenth Cavalry and again from 1886 to 1889 (the longest tenure of any officer who commanded Fort Hays), when he was a colonel in the Eighteenth Infantry. He died at Fort Hays, February 17, 1889. The regimental band played while his body was transported to the railroad depot in Hays City to be taken east for burial. As the procession moved through Hays City the band played the "Dead March."

Marcus A. Reno had a distinguished Civil War career before he was appointed major in the Seventh Cavalry in 1868. He commanded Fort Hays several different times during 1870 and 1871. Because of the controversy surrounding his role in the Battle of the Little Big Horn in 1876, Reno eventually was dismissed from the service in 1880.

by Indians at Beecher's Island on the Arikaree Fork of the Republican River in eastern Colorado in September 1868. They were rescued nine days later, but had suffered several casualties. Sheridan abandoned that experiment. But his other innovation, the winter campaign of 1868–1869, carried destruction and defeat to some of the tribes. Fort Hays contributed to the success of that campaign by receiving vital supplies via the railroad and forwarding them by wagon train to Fort Dodge and Camp Supply, Indian Territory, where they were sent to troops in the field.

Lieutenant Colonel Custer was returned to duty at Sheridan's request even though his one-year suspension from the service was not up, and Custer led his regiment in an attack on a Cheyenne village on the Washita River in present-day Oklahoma, November 27, 1868. In addition to capturing Black Kettle's camp, destroying Indians' homes and supplies, and killing a large pony herd, Custer's force took more than fifty Indian captives.

The Cheyenne captives were brought to Fort Hays and confined in a special "Indian pen" constructed against the old post guardhouse. The pen enclosed an area 58 by 186 feet, had walls fourteen feet high with observation walks for guards, and contained seven tents to house fifty-three prisoners (fifty women and children and three men). An unfortunate incident occurred with these prisoners in May 1869 when the three males were being moved and apparently believed they were going to be executed. They resisted, a fight followed, and two of the men prisoners, possibly one of the women prisoners, and the sergeant of the guard were killed. The remaining captives stayed at Fort Hays until June 13, 1869, when they were returned to their people on the reservation in Indian Territory. Meanwhile, Custer and the Seventh Cavalry encamped near Fort Hays along Big Creek and helped protect the railroad and settlers of the region. The Seventh Cavalry went to Fort Leavenworth during the winter of 1869–1870 and returned to camp near Fort Hays again during the spring and summer of 1870. Although Custer was never a part of the Fort Hays garrison, he was closely associated with the fort during those years.

Indian resistance in western Kansas continued at high levels in 1869, keeping the Fort Hays troops fully occupied, but thereafter Indian raids declined considerably as the natives were forced to accept their reservations. The last Indian scare in western Kansas occurred in 1878 but did not directly affect Fort Hays.

Fort Hays remained an active post for another decade after 1878 to provide security for the settlement of the western Kansas Plains. Indians were forced to abandon their traditional way of life because the coming of the railroad had led to the destruction of the buffalo herds, building of towns, occupation of homesteads, and the efficiency of the military arm used against them. With their passing, the military need for Fort Hays was finished, but the post remained for a time to assure everyone that the change in population was permanent.

General Philip H. Sheridan, famous Civil War commander, replaced Hancock as commander of the Department of the Missouri in late 1867. In preparation for the winter campaign against Indian camps in present-day Oklahoma, Sheridan established his headquarters at Fort Hays in the summer of 1868. He later moved to Fort Dodge and, when the troops moved into Oklahoma, to Camp Supply. His confidence in George A. Custer as an Indian fighter was rewarded with the victory at the Battle of the Washita in November 1868 and the surrender of many Indians thereafter. Sheridan's plan to destroy the Indians' winter camps proved to be a major step toward ending Indian domination on the Plains. Sheridan became general-in-chief of the army in 1883 and held that post until his death in 1888.

Lieutenant Colonel Eugene A. Carr, Fifth Cavalry, commanded Fort Hays in 1875 and 1876. He had received the Congressional Medal of Honor for valor during the Civil War, and he had defeated an encampment of Cheyenne Dog Soldiers under Chief Tall Bull at Summit Springs, Colorado Territory, in July 1869. In the summer of 1876 Carr and his regiment left the Southwest. The story of his life is told in James T. King, War Eagle: A Life of General Eugene A. Carr *(1963).*

During its occupation, Fort Hays was commanded by fifty-two officers, several of whom served more than once, including John E. Yard, Samuel Ovenshine, Nelson A. Miles, Marcus A. Reno, William B. Hazen, E. A. Carr, Richard I. Dodge, and many lesser-known officers. As noted, George A. Custer was encamped near the fort in 1867, 1869, and 1870, but was never a part of the garrison. His brother Tom Custer was on several occasions assigned to duty at Fort Hays, as were many other Seventh Cavalry officers. (For a complete list of commanding officers see Appendix.)

The garrison usually consisted of both cavalry and infantry companies and sometimes was supplemented with an artillery battery. Its size varied considerably, from a high of 568 officers and enlisted men during the height of Indian troubles in August 1867 to a low of only 17 men from May to September 1879. Black troops were present when black regiment companies (Thirty-eighth Infantry and Ninth and Tenth Cavalries) were stationed at the post from January 1867 to April 1869 and from December 1881 to May 1885. For a short time the garrison comprised mostly black soldiers, as in August 1867 when 472 of 545 enlisted men belonged to black regiments. All black regiments had white officers. Conversely, no black troops were at Fort Hays during seventeen of the twenty-five years it was occupied. Black soldiers performed admirably during the era of the Indian wars in the West, and their regiments, despite the racism encountered among white soldiers and civilians, had fewer disciplinary problems, the lowest desertion rate, and the highest rate of reenlistment in the entire army.

Nevertheless, the presence of black troops at Fort Hays led to racial problems in the community. In 1867 three black soldiers were refused entrance to a local house of prostitution. Probably intoxicated and angered by this treatment, they vowed to kill the first white man they saw. They entered Tommy Drum's famous saloon in Hays City and shot John Hays, a civilian employee of the fort who was helping guard military stores that had been unloaded from the railroad and were awaiting transport to the post warehouses. The three soldiers later were identified at the fort, and the county sheriff arrested and jailed them in town. There the blacks were seized by an angry mob, taken to the railroad bridge west of town, and hanged.

In the fall of 1869 several black soldiers were killed in a fight they started after being denied entrance to a saloon in Hays City. The other black troops in this fight were driven back to the

Richard I. Dodge graduated from West Point in 1848 and remained in the service until retirement in 1891. He was a lieutenant colonel in the Twenty-third Infantry when he commanded Fort Hays in 1878 and 1879. He served at a number of western forts and was a student of the region and Indians. He published The Plains of the Great West *(1877) and* Thirty-three Years Among Our Wild Indians *(1882).*

fort by a citizen mob. In 1882 several black soldiers were arrested for disturbing the peace, and one was killed by a local law officer for resisting arrest. When word of this incident reached the post, a large group of black soldiers went into town determined to kill the officer responsible for the death of their friend, but post commander Captain Lloyd Wheaton intervened and persuaded the soldiers to return to the fort without their intended revenge.

It should be noted that a number of soldiers, black and white, became involved in fights when they were in Hays City. Their drinking, gambling, and visits to houses of prostitution created situations in which troopers got into arguments and fights with civilians and with each other. Hays City had a reputation for being a wild town, and the soldiers — along with railroad workers, cattlemen, gamblers, and prostitutes — contributed their share to that image. Most of the trouble with soldiers in town occurred soon after payday while the men still had a few dollars to spend for recreation and dissipation.

Nelson A. Miles compiled a fine record during the Civil War and was awarded the Congressional Medal of Honor for gallantry during the Battle of Chancellorsville. He was a colonel in the Fifth Infantry when he commanded Fort Hays in 1869 during the time the Cheyenne prisoners were incarcerated there. He and George A. Custer hunted buffalo together near the post. Miles later played a major role in several Indian campaigns, including the defeat of the Nez Perce, Sioux, and Geronimo's Apaches. He rose to the rank of general and was commander-in-chief of the army from 1895 until his retirement in 1903. Of the many commanders of Fort Hays, he is probably the best known for his overall military record.

7

Economic Concerns

The soldiers' pay was only a small portion of the money that benefited the local economy because of the presence of a military post, and those salaries alone at Fort Hays amounted to thousands of dollars each month. How enlisted men and officers spent their pay is difficult to accurately determine, but that most of it ended up in the coffers of local merchants (including the post sutler, general stores in town, saloons, and bordellos) is certain. An enlisted man's pay was not large, ranging from thirteen dollars per month for a new private to about thirty dollars per month for a noncommissioned officer with several years' service. Officers' pay began at a base of $150 per month during the post-Civil War years, and some officers received expense accounts in addition to salaries.

Since most of a soldier's necessities were furnished by his employer, his pay was available for "luxuries." A soldier needed money only when he was stationed at the post, for there was no place to spend it while in the field on a campaign. If a soldier hired a company laundress to keep his clothes and bedding clean, the fixed charge at Fort Hays was one dollar per month for all laundry except an overcoat, pair of pants, and bed-sack, for which there was an additional charge of twenty-five cents each. Laundresses' charges could be avoided if the soldier cared to take his own hands and clothes to the washboard. Some soldiers cut each other's hair, saving the twenty-five cents for a trim or fifty cents for the works at a barbershop in town. What monthly pay remained could be used for a variety

The post trader's store was the only civilian establishment permitted on a military reservation. The post trader or sutler had a contract with the army to operate his store in return for a specified annual payment. Prices charged at the store were determined by a board of officers who permitted a certain markup over cost for the items sold. Fort Hays had one of the finest sutler's stores in the West, and it had an officers' club room where officers could drink, play cards, shoot billiards, and visit. In one area enlisted men could purchase beer and liquor, gamble, and relax. The store, open to officers and enlisted men and their families, offered a wide choice of items. The following is a partial list of items and prices at a post near Fort Hays in 1863, illustrative of the kinds of products offered and the cost of living at a western army post during the Civil War years. (The sizes of cans, bottles, and boxes listed are unknown.)

Potatoes, per bushel	$2.25	Beer, per gallon	$1.00
Apples, per bushel	3.50	Whiskey, per gallon	1.50
Flour, per sack	4.75	Crackers, per pound	.13
Tomatoes, per can	.60	Corn Meal, per pound	.04
Peaches, per can	.85	Butter, per pound	.25
Strawberries, per can	.85	Chocolate, per pound	.50
Oysters, per can	.75	Brown Sugar, per pound	.18
Lobsters, per can	.50	Cheese, per pound	.22
Pineapple, per can	.85	Tea, per pound	1.25
Jelly, per can	.75	Chewing Tobacco, per pound	.90
Coffee, per box	.45	Mixed Candy, per pound	.60
Clothes Pins, per box	2.50	Soap, per pound	.30
Cigars, per box	4.50	Playing Cards, pack	.25
Eggs, per dozen	.30	Diaper Pins, @	.25
Tomato Catsup, per bottle	.20	Neckties, @	.30

Castor Oil, per bottle ...... *.25*	*Candles, @* .... *.25*
Cologne, per bottle .... *.25*	*Wash Boards, @* *1.00*
Blue Jean Pants, per pair .. *4.75*	*Hoop Skirts, @* *2.50*
Canvas, per yard .... *.25*	*Lead Pencils, @* .... *.10*
Blankets, ... *11.00-15.00*	*Smoking Pipes @* *1.10-7.50*

Other items included song books, fishhooks, coffee pots, guitar strings, saddles, lanterns, Epsom salt, cloth, pots and pans, hats, matches, needles and thread, spices, nails, revolvers, buttons, sulphur, hair dye, turpentine, wallets, tin buckets, molasses, axes, padlocks, scissors, mirrors, beads, and horse liniment.

of purchases; rarely does it appear that any of it was saved, although many soldiers did send some of their pay home to their needy families.

The troops usually were paid in cash every other month, but occasionally the paymaster's visit came only once in four or even six months. This made payday an even more important event to celebrate, and the accumulation of several months' pay gave the soldiers a fairly large sum with which to slake the thirst of a long dry spell. The spree after payday often brought the work of the garrison almost to a standstill. There was debate among military leaders regarding the frequency of pay.

Hill P. Wilson was the post trader at Fort Hays for a number of years. He was a successful business manager who also built and operated stores in Hays City. He built one of the historic structures in Hays in 1874 where he operated a general store and where the U.S. Land Office was located for a short time. It still stands at the corner of Eighth and Main Streets in Hays and houses the Philip and Son Hardware business (in operation there since 1896). Wilson built other businesses in Hays and was an early promoter of the town.

The quartermaster was in charge of equipment, supplies, and transportation at the post, and he also oversaw construction and repairs of buildings. This 1873 photo shows (1) the office of the post quartermaster, (2) quarters for the noncommissioned quartermaster staff, (3) three quartermaster warehouses, each ninety-six by twenty-four feet, connected to each other by a covered passageway ten feet wide, (4) quartermaster shops (including blacksmith, wheelwright, carpenter, and saddler), and (5) wagon shed. In addition the quartermaster also had corrals and other storage units under his jurisdiction. Because he was responsible for a large inventory and considerable monetary accounts, the quartermaster held one of the most demanding positions at the fort. Since he was in charge of the physical plant, his favors often were curried by officers and their wives. The comfort and well-being of the garrison depended largely upon the capabilities of the quartermaster.

In 1867 the adjutant general reported: "It has been suggested by many intelligent officers that more frequent payments would tend to diminish brawls and desertions and temptation to intemperance, by keeping the men more constantly supplied with such small sums as they need for the moderate wants of themselves or families, instead of throwing in their hands comparatively large sums sometimes the accumulated pay of six months." The inspector general argued the other side: "The longer you keep soldiers' pay, the longer you prevent them from desertion, and the more seldom they are paid, the fewer drunken irregularities will occur." The paymaster general objected to frequent payments on the grounds that the soldiers never would have enough money at one

The commissary warehouse, located northeast of the parade ground, was where the food supply was stored. This building (150 by 34 feet) had a basement for additional storage space. The building was carefully secured (note the bars over some of the windows) because the temptation to steal food was great; many enlisted men considered their daily rations inadequate. They could purchase additional food at the post trader's store, but low pay and other demands for their money (such as liquor and gambling) often made such supplemental food purchases impossible. The alternative was to appropriate some of the commissary stores after hours. In addition to security, a major worry of the commissary officer (sometimes the quartermaster also served this duty in addition to all his others) was spoilage of food on the shelf. Before any food could be thrown out as unfit for consumption, a board of officers would have to meet and determine that the food was spoiled. This building was kept in good repair. In 1887 it was declared to be the best structure on the post.

time to send any home to their families. The pay schedule remained unchanged, and the soldiers continued to spend their pay at local establishments whenever they had it.

Because of insufficient military manpower to provide all services needed by the army, such as scouting, hauling supplies, herding livestock, cutting firewood, repairing buildings and equipment, keeping records, and similar tasks, civilian employees always were present at Fort Hays. During the peak years of military activity at the post, from 1867 to 1870, the number of civilians hired varied from fewer than twenty during early 1868 to more than four hundred during the winter campaign of 1868–1869. The largest monthly civilian payroll at the fort was

Another view of the forage house and corrals, depicting a large number of horses and mules as well as a supply train of canvas-covered wagons.

for December 1868, with $23,132.25 dispensed into the local economy through a host of clerks, guides, couriers, teamsters, laborers, herdsmen, watchmen, blacksmiths, wheelwrights, and others. At the other extreme in March 1868 the total civilian payroll at the fort was only $598.92. The average monthly civilian payroll during the peak years noted above was $7,528.14.

The need for civilian workers declined after Indian removal and the size of the garrison was reduced, but such employees were present until the abandonment of the post. From 1867 to 1889 the average monthly civilian payroll was $1,550.60. Thus the fort was a significant contributor to the local economy for more than twenty years. It must be assumed that most of the civilian employees, as did the soldiers, spent their pay for the necessities and luxuries provided by local businesses.

This 1873 photo shows (1) the forage house where hay and grain for draft animals was stored, (2) the hay yard where prairie hay was stacked during the summer to provide food for livestock during the winter, and (3) the lower mule corral. These were all under the quartermaster's jurisdiction.

In addition to the salaries, large sums were spent to purchase supplies in the region for troops' use. Whenever possible, fresh vegetables, grain, milk, eggs, and other items were to be purchased from the community near a fort in order to save transportation costs. All items that could not be found locally had to be shipped in at great expense.

Military supplies usually reached Fort Leavenworth on the Missouri River by steamboat, but they had to be hauled from that point by rail and wagon to western forts. Freighting military supplies was big business, for the freight charges often were greater than the cost of the products being freighted. The numerous employees of freighting firms held jobs because of the army, and many of those employees later became settlers in the West. The railroad, which arrived early in the history of Fort Hays, derived much of its business as well as protection from the army. Because new railroads crossing the Plains faced enormous construction costs and had to await the settlement of the region through which they passed before much freight was generated by the civilian populace, they depended on army freight to help pay the bills during those early years.

In these and other ways, the federal money spent on a military installation bolstered the community economy. Then as now it was economically desirable to have an army base nearby. Because of the economic benefits, it is understandable that communities located near a post wanted the garrison to remain long after the troops had fulfilled their military mission. This was true of Fort Hays, which was maintained for more than a decade after Indians had departed from the region.

8

Life at the Fort

The life of the soldier at Fort Fletcher and Old Fort Hays, 1865–1867, was one of isolation, since no civilian community was nearby. In addition, duties were monotonous and living conditions were poor. Housed first in tents, which often were blown down by the proverbial Kansas winds, and later in crude huts, which they had constructed as part of their duty assignment, the soldiers had neither comfortable quarters nor many conveniences. Their food was often of poor quality because it had been transported over vast distances, and it was sometimes spoiled because of improper storage and the length of time in transit and storage before consumption. Some of the hardtack was left over from the Civil War; Custer declared that some bread issued to his regiment in 1867 had been baked and boxed in 1861. Sometimes the salt pork was rancid, and the flour often had worms in it before it was used.

The soldiers' diet had little variety. Hash, stew, bread, salt pork, and beans were standard items, and coffee and sugar were included in the rations. Fresh meat often was available, sometimes from freshly slaughtered beef and sometimes from buffalo. Most of this meat was served in stew, usually accompanied by some canned vegetables. Each company was responsible for feeding its own troopers, and soldiers ate at a company mess hall located behind each barracks. Meals were prepared by cooks of various talents since they were selected from within the company without regard to previous experience. While at the post, the men also had the daily bread from the post bakery. Troops in the field prepared their own mess

Fort Hays was known as a four-company post because it had barracks for four companies of troops, each company comprising up to one hundred men when at full strength. The four buildings were on three sides of the parade ground; the officers' houses were on the other side. Each barracks was 118 feet long by 24 feet wide and was divided into two dormitories, one fifty-five by twenty-four feet and the other forty-two by twenty-four feet. In addition the first sergeant's room was thirteen by thirteen feet, and there was a storeroom, eleven by thirteen feet. Men slept in double two-tier bunks, two men on the bottom and two on the top. In 1874 these bunks were replaced with single-man iron beds. The buildings were heated in winter by stoves, first burning wood and later coal, and were ventilated by opening the windows. Kitchens and mess halls were contained in separate buildings located behind each barracks. The quarters for married soldiers were provided in four frame buildings located at the southeast corner of the building complex. Each building contained four sets of quarters of two rooms each, each room only twelve feet square. The wives of enlisted men often were employed as laundresses at the post.

individually and generally had poorer quality vittles except for the fresh game they hunted. The lack of fresh vegetables in the diet was a problem, and scurvy was a disease that plagued the troops in those early years.

The move to the new location near the railroad in 1867 brought considerable improvement in conditions, especially when the new barracks, kitchens, mess halls, bakery, and storage facilities were completed. In addition the fort's isolation ended with the rise of towns nearby, beginning with Rome on the same side of Big Creek and later Hays City across the creek.

With the railroad towns came merchants, saloons, prostitutes, and gamblers, all of which provided a chance to escape the routines of post life. A pass was required to leave the post and visit the outside community, but soldiers often were found absent without leave enjoying the offerings available.

Desertion was a common way to escape permanently from military duty, and the number who deserted was high throughout the years Fort Hays was an active post. Some deserters were caught and punished but most

Officers' row formed the south side of the parade ground and eventually contained ten houses, nine of which can be seen in this 1873 photograph. The houses were not all alike, and the two on the right were constructed later than the other seven shown (a photo taken in 1869 shows only seven houses). The tenth house was the chaplain's home at the left of this photo (not visible). The commanding officer's quarters (fourth building from the left) contained four rooms, each fifteen by thirteen feet, a kitchen attached to the rear (seventeen by thirteen feet), and four attic rooms for servants' use for storage. Most of the other structures housed two officers and their families who shared kitchen facilities attached to the rear. Officer housing was selected by rank, and any officer who outranked another could "bump" the lower-ranking officer from his quarters. With the high turnover among officers at the post, considerable moving occurred. Each officer who was "bumped" could "bump" any officer of lower rank, and the result was like musical chairs. If all officer quarters were occupied, the lowest ranking officer might be found living in a tent. Two houses, the first and second from the left in this photo, have been restored on their original locations as a part of Fort Hays State Historic Site.

These two views of officers' row, above taken in 1869 and below in 1885, depict the improvements that occurred over the years. The top photo, taken two years after the fort was occupied, shows the basic structures on the open prairie. The Fifth Infantry band with instruments stands on the parade ground. The bottom photo includes some alterations and the additions of trees and shrubs as well as some fences. Certainly the later place looks more pleasant as a home.

made good their escape. In 1867 throughout the entire army there were 13,608 desertions from a total enlistment of 53,962. In that year the Seventh Cavalry, serving in the region of Fort Hays, lost 457 to desertion out of a total of 865 enlisted men. Cavalry regiments had more desertions than the infantry because cavalrymen could use their horses to get away.

The desertion rate was very high during the era of the western Indian wars. Secretary of War Stephen B. Elkins reported in 1891 that one-third of

The hospital complex was surrounded by a picket fence. The main ward of this prefabricated pine hospital is on the left; it was forty by twenty-four feet. The smaller ward in the building in the center was twenty-eight by twenty-four feet, but this building also contained the surgeon's office (twelve by nine feet) and a dispensary (twelve by seven feet). These two buildings were connected by a fourteen-by-twelve-foot passageway. A kitchen and dining room were attached to the rear of the main ward. The hospital steward lived in the small house seen behind the wards. The small structure with only the roof visible at the right was the dead house where a corpse was kept until interment in the post cemetery or shipment to another cemetery. A post surgeon's home was built later between the hospital and the blockhouse. Before that house was constructed, the post surgeon had quarters on officers' row. Two other features of the hospital not shown were a garden to produce fresh vegetables for the hospital mess and an outhouse. The post hospital aided civilian as well as military personnel and was the finest and best-equipped hospital in the region as long as the post was active.

The Seventh Cavalry encamped near Fort Hays along the banks of Big Creek during the spring and summer of 1869. Seen here is a portion of the camp with trees along the creek in the background.

This view of the Seventh Cavalry camp shows some of the troops at attention during an evening dress parade in 1869.

the men recruited between 1867 and the year of his report had deserted. Many reasons have been given to explain desertions. Among the most important were general dissatisfaction with military life, the length of enlistment (all soldiers were volunteers and were in for five years), harsh discipline of troops, inadequate pay and the hope of making more money elsewhere, boresome garrison life, the temptation to go to the gold mines, inferior quarters, inferior and insufficient food, and the use of troops for nonmilitary purposes such as building shelters and roads. Fear of disease during an epidemic and fear of death while on an Indian campaign also caused individuals to decide to depart and not return. Many soldiers apparently departed while under the influence of alcohol, so drinking was another contributing factor. That only 30 percent of those who deserted were apprehended, and many of them were returned to duty with only slight punishment, must have encouraged would-be deserters. In most instances it was likely a combination of reasons that provoked a soldier to desert.

Desertion was not considered a serious crime in those days, but the army tried to stop it because it represented an economic loss. Deserters almost always took government property with them when they departed, some of which they sold and some of which they used for their own welfare. Also, since deserters had to be replaced, it added greatly to the cost of recruiting and training new soldiers. Even so, effective means for preventing widespread desertion were not devised until the twentieth century.

There were many desertions from Fort Hays, but the rate was higher at more isolated posts and among troops on campaigns. Those soldiers who served out their five-year enlistment found their daily lives at Fort Hays organized into a rigid routine. The schedule varied from season to season, from commanding officer to commanding officer, and depending on the units stationed at the post (when no cavalry were present, for example, there would be no stable call), but a typical day's routine when cavalrymen were present went somewhat as follows:

The first call for reveille was sounded at 5:45 a.m. and reveille was at 5:55, with assembly for roll call at 6:00. Mess call for breakfast was at 6:15. At 7:00 came stable call, when the men of the cavalry went to the stables, cleaned them, and took the horses to water. If there was to be mounted drill during the morning (this usually happened only two or three days a week), the horses were taken back to the stables; otherwise the animals were sent out under a mounted guard to graze at some selected spot on the military reservation and within bugle call from the post headquarters.

Fatigue call was sounded at 7:30 a.m.; the men detailed from each company for such jobs as cleaning up the post, working on a construction site,

Custer's camp near Fort Hays in 1869, with Mrs. Custer (seated second from left) and George Custer (standing to right of center tent pole) with several guests. This complex of tents provided them several rooms in which to live and entertain, including a guest room.

loading or unloading supplies, building a road, cutting ice, and numerous other duties were assembled at the guardhouse where they departed for their respective duties under the charge of a noncommissioned officer. Sick call also was sounded at 7:30, and all men who were ailing in any of the companies were sent to the post hospital to be examined by the post surgeon and treated accordingly. If nothing wrong was found, the soldier was sent to join the fatigue detail to which he had been assigned. If his affliction was minor, he was sent to quarters. A serious ailment resulted in his admission to the hospital for observation and treatment.

At 8:00 a.m. the new guard for the day was called to assemble at the guardhouse where he stood inspection, including performance of all or part of the manual of arms. The orders for the day and the passwords were given, and the new guard relieved the old guard for a twenty-four-hour shift. Enlisted men were assigned to guard duty by some system of rotation. They had to remain fully dressed throughout the twenty-four-hour period while performing various duties. Sentinels were stationed at key posts on the fort where they were relieved every two hours. Sentinels were required to challenge intruders, call out their post number and the time every hour, and repeat the orders of the day upon the request of an officer. Sometimes guards would be in charge of prisoners from the guardhouse who were required to work at some job around the post. When a guard had rest time, he spent it in the guard room of the guardhouse.

Sometimes quarters were insufficient for everyone in the post garrison. The overflow lived in tents, as shown here with an unidentified soldier and his family.

If there was a morning drill the recall from fatigue details was sounded at 9:45 a.m. and the drill was called at 10:00. Recall from drill usually was at 11:30, although cavalrymen were sometimes not recalled until 11:45. Mess call for dinner was at 12:00 noon. Afternoon fatigue call sounded at 1:00 p.m.; if afternoon drills were scheduled fatigue details were recalled and sent to drill at 2:00. Recall from fatigue on days when there was no drill, or from drill, came at 4:30. At 4:45 came stable call again, when cavalrymen groomed the horses.

The troops were called to assembly at 5:30 p.m., with the evening dress parade and roll call at 5:40. Dress parade ended the working day at the fort. The evening mess was at 6:30. Tattoo was sounded at 9:30; this was the last roll call of the day, with the soldiers in company formations in front of their quarters. Lights were to be out when taps sounded at 10:00.

Throughout the day, whenever a soldier was not answering a call, on fatigue detail, or at drill, he was free to go to his barracks or anywhere on the post as long as he was within bugle call. The routine on Sunday was different, for there were no work details or drill, except for those on guard duty. A weekly inspection of the troops was held at dress parade at 9:00 a.m. on Sunday, after which the men were free until tattoo.

Men who followed the prescribed routine, reported for duty, and performed their assignments — the bulk of the troops — had free time for diversion and entertainment. Those who failed to perform were placed in confinement. How the former spent their free time varied widely: some spent time in conversation with other men in the same company; some read newspapers and books from the post library; some wrote letters and kept diaries. Others competed in contests including horse races, foot races, pitching horseshoes, and baseball games, and some of the men were fond of betting on the outcome. All types of gambling — including cards and dice — occupied many troopers. Card games also were played for pleasure. Some of the men had musical instruments and some men sang, entertaining themselves and those who listened. Practical jokes always were popular, especially upon new recruits. Sometimes a group of men would venture into drama and produce a play for the garrison's entertainment. When regimental bands were stationed at the fort, the soldiers spent many hours listening to the musicians perform.

Fort Hays had several regimental bands stationed there at various times, and those bands performed many official and unofficial functions. They played at dress parades and inspections, and they gave concerts on and off the post, played for dances, and at other times provided entertainment. They were good for public relations, as they often were called upon to play off the post, and they were applauded by civilians wherever they went.

The *Hays Sentinel* reported in February 1876, "The Fifth Cavalry Band have returned from their eastern trip. They created quite a sensation; and the general verdict was, that never had such music been heard before. The citizens of Lawrence, Topeka and Leavenworth were enraptured with their playing, and have engaged them for some forthcoming festivities. They deserve all the credit that can be bestowed upon them." This same band performed in the centennial celebration of the nation's birth on July 4, 1876, in Topeka. In later years the Eighteenth Infantry band was stationed at Fort Hays until the post was abandoned. When the band departed, the editor of the Hays City *Republican* wrote: "In losing the 18th Infantry Band, the people of Hays lose something that can never be replaced. Such sweet music

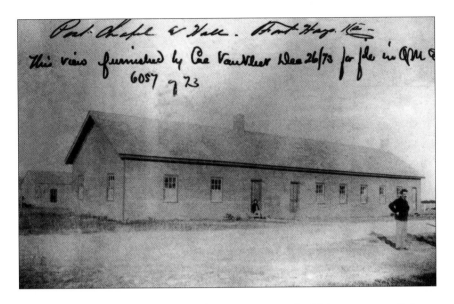

The post chapel served numerous functions, most of which were not religious. It was sometimes a school for children on the post, often a dance hall for the officers and their ladies, and usually was occupied by any band stationed at the post (bandsmen practiced, gave concerts, and played for the dances). This building came to Fort Hays because the officers' wives were determined to have a dance hall. Fort Hays had a chaplain but no chapel, and there was a chapel at the abandoned Fort Harker. The ladies had the post commander request authority to move the chapel to Hays. This was accomplished, and the ladies had their dance hall. The chaplain held religious services there too.

very few western cities have ever had. The boys were kind, liberal and courteous, playing for our citizens very often."

Life is more than work and play, even at a frontier military post, and illnesses and injuries were a constant threat to the army. The post surgeon and his hospital were important to the health and well being of the garrison. Many health problems were environmental: crowded and poorly ventilated quarters fostered respiratory illnesses, unsanitary water induced diarrhea and fevers, mosquitoes along Big Creek carried malarial afflictions, inadequate bathing facilities contributed to numerous boils, and the local prostitutes spread venereal diseases. A ready supply of liquor at the "whiskey ranches" and local saloons contributed to alcoholism and influenced many fights. Some soldiers were hospitalized for gunshot wounds, few of which were inflicted by Indians. Some resulted from fights in town with other sol-

The Eighteenth Infantry band was stationed at Fort Hays from May 18, 1886, until September 29, 1889. The band was very popular at the fort and in Hays City where it often played. Band members and the instruments they played when this photo was taken in 1886 were (the names are not in the same order as the men appear in the picture):

Theodore Wurm, leader,
  solo Bb cornet
August Kung, Eb clarinet
Edward Harvey, Bb clarinet
Franz Schenring, Bb clarinet
Michael McGuffin, Bb clarinet
Charles Smitz, Bb clarinet
Oscar Grett, Eb cornet
Charles Sherwood, Bb cornet
Jonas B. Adams, Bb cornet
Louis Witt, Bb cornet

Jeremiah Ryan, Bb cornet
Will C. Smitt, solo Alto
Aaron Middleton, first alto
James Maxwell, second alto
Fritz Guenther, first trombone
Emil Klausmeyer, second trombone
Frank Ehrenfried, baritone
James Lancaster, Eb tuba
John Keisenwetter, Eb tuba
Fred Liley, snare drum
Edw. Stein, bass drum

diers or civilians, quite a few from accidents, and a few were self-inflicted. Cavalrymen often were injured by their horses. There were a few outbreaks of the dreaded cholera, most notably in 1867 during the peak of Indian troubles and while the railroad was under construction in the region.

The cholera epidemic of 1867 was widespread, covering most of western Kansas, eastern Colorado, and other points along the overland routes of travel. The first case appeared at Fort Hays on July 11, 1867, but the civilian community suffered more losses to this disease than did the army. Both civilians and soldiers were treated at the post hospital, which at that time was housed in tents. During that epidemic, which lasted through August, a total of 36 soldiers died at the post and an estimated 150 civilians in the community.

Cholera, which is contracted from an infected water supply, results in rapid dehydration of the body. Copious vomiting, diarrhea, and kidney failure were usual symptoms, and the death rate was often as high as 50 percent, most deaths occurring within twenty-four hours after the first symptoms appeared. Those who recovered usually were over the illness within three to five days. The cholera epidemic was a factor in the large number of desertions experienced in 1867.

During the epidemic at the post, a quarantine ward was set up in tents, and the hospital staff was supplemented with five privates from the guard-

During the years of Indian conflict soldiers stationed at Fort Hays were kept busy with military operations off post. But after the Indian wars during the last dozen years of the fort's existence, life at the post could be routine and boring. Still the soldiers ate well, enjoyed the benefits of town life in Hays City, and had leisure hours to spend as they pleased. One recreational activity enjoyed in that area was hunting buffalo. This photograph of a group of buffalo hunters was taken near Fort Hays in 1869.

house. The soldiers who died were buried in the post cemetery and later removed, along with others interred there, to the national cemetery at Fort Leavenworth several years after Fort Hays was abandoned.

Cholera claimed many victims, but other types of medical problems, such as sprains, blisters, cuts, bruises, colds, influenza, broken bones, and many other ailments required the attention of the medical staff. The post surgeon and hospital attendants were responsible for diagnosis, treatment, and surgery when necessary, and their activities included such health-related duties as sanitation, diet, examination of recruits, and the maintenance of medical records. The post surgeon also was required to administer the hospital, supervise all other medical personnel, dispense drugs, act as post coroner, keep zoological and botanical records for the region, and record daily weather conditions.

This photograph taken on North Main Street in Hays City confirms the image of the town as lawless and that Fort Hays's soldiers died from causes other than Indian conflicts or disease. The dead men, Privates Peter Walsh and George Summer, Sixth Cavalry, were shot by one of their fellow troopers, David Roberts, on September 6, 1873.

With so many duties, it was necessary that the post surgeon have hospital attendants to help. Their duties involved nurse care for the sick and wounded, meal preparation, provision of proper diet, changing bandages, and bathing hospital patients when necessary. These attendants were assigned hospital duty on a rotation basis from the companies stationed at the fort, thus most were inexperienced when assigned to duty and were rotated off duty about the time they gained essential experience with their tasks. Post surgeons often complained about the attendant selection system, emphasizing that it was detrimental to the patients, but to no avail.

Because diet is so important to health (for example, Vitamin C deficiency causes scurvy), military posts were required to plant gardens to provide fresh vegetables. Fort Hays had company gardens and a hospital garden, but these often failed as a result of adverse weather conditions, insects, and lack of interest. It was only after the military activity decreased that more time was spent with the post gardens and more favorable results were reported.

In spite of all the problems noted, it appears that the health of the Fort Hays garrison generally was good and the health care provided was adequate. If cleanliness could have been better enforced, many of the ailments that did flourish would have been reduced considerably. There is no record of any bathing facilities at the fort until the last decade of its occupation.

Just as soldiers neglected their physical well-being, they had little interest in the spiritual side of life. Fort Hays had a chaplain during much of its existence, and it provided a chapel after 1872, but it was mainly officers and their families who attended religious services. Formal religion was apparently not very significant to most enlisted men. The post chapel attracted more of them to the school sessions available in the evenings than it did to Sunday morning worship.

Fort Hays provided a school for the soldiers who wished to learn to read and write and perform elementary mathematical functions. At times post children were provided with a day school, and the enlisted men attended in the evenings. Some years, however, the children at the fort were sent to the public school in Hays City. At the post school the chaplain was sometimes the teacher; at other times an enlisted man taught for a little extra pay. (In 1872 he received six dollars extra each month.) Since many of the soldiers were recent immigrants — chiefly from Ireland, Germany, and Great Britain — and many of the native-born were illiterate, those who

William A. Comstock
(1842–1868)

Civilian Scouts

Moses E. Milner
(1829–1876)

William F. Cody
(1846–1917)

Civilian scouts were hired to assist the army; these men served as scouts in and around Fort Hays at various times.

*James B. Hickok
(1837–1876)*

*Simpson E. Stilwell
(1849–1903)*

*Allison J. Pliley
(1844–1917)*

desired to improve themselves took advantage of this program to learn basic skills.

Life at Fort Hays during the years of Indian troubles, especially the late 1860s and early 1870s, usually was filled with some activity related to military operations off the post. The scouting expeditions, patrols along transportation routes, guard duty at a stage station or railroad construction camp, or a campaign against hostile Indians were all welcome relief from the monotony of garrison life. After the Indian wars, during the last dozen years of the fort's existence, life at the post was even more routine and boring. The garrison was small, few opportunities existed for service in the field, and much of the work involved the maintenance of a post that was built for temporary duty and was in constant need of repairs. Some buildings fell into disuse, and others were not repaired as they deteriorated. Even so, life was easier for the soldiers. They ate well, enjoyed the benefits of town life in Hays City, had access to the rest of the nation via the railroad, and leisure hours to spend as they pleased, reading a newspaper, writing to family and friends back home, or sitting on the bank of Big Creek. During those last years life at the post was quite different from life during the frontier era; Fort Hays was a small village near a larger town that was a vestige of an earlier time when the federal government provided protective assistance to the settlement of the land.

9

Fort Hays Today

Fort Hays officially was closed on November 8, 1889, and the military reservation and fort structures were turned over to the Department of the Interior. Military stores were shipped to other posts. A decade later Congress transferred the land to the State of Kansas to be used for a branch of the state agricultural college, a branch of the normal school, and a public park; all three are still in operation. The Kansas State University Agricultural Research Center (formerly known as the Fort Hays Experiment Station), is the largest dryland experiment station in the world. Many crop and livestock developments have resulted from the research conducted there. Fort Hays State University, the only state university in the western half of Kansas, has evolved from the western branch of the Kansas State Normal School, which began conducting classes in the old fort hospital in 1902 and later moved to the site of the present campus on the former military reservation. Fort Hays State Historic Site, administered by the Kansas State Historical Society, contains a modern visitor's center and four of the original fort buildings: the stone blockhouse, stone guardhouse, and two of the frame officers' quarters. The fine exhibits of this museum portray the history of a fort that assisted travelers and traders, stagelines and railroads, miners and cowboys, buffalo hunters and farmers, merchants and other settlers who occupied the West.

At the end of the nineteenth century Congress transferred the Fort Hays military reservation land to the State of Kansas to be used for an agricultural experiment station, a college, and a park. The Kansas State University Agricultural Research Center (above) is the largest dryland experiment station in the world. Fort Hays State University (below) is the only state university in the western half of Kansas.

Fort Hays State Historic Site comprises a modern visitor's center and four original fort buildings. Museum exhibits portray the history of Fort Hays from its establishment in 1865 to 1889 when the fort was abandoned as an active post. In this photo the rehabilitated blockhouse stands in the background, and a reconstructed well house is in the foreground.

Restored officers' quarters, Fort Hays State Historic Site.

Appendix

Report on Fort Hays Flood

Post Quartermaster Captain Sam B. Lauffler filed the following report of the flood that swept through Old Fort Hays during the night of June 7, 1867:

> On the night of the 7th inst. this place was visited by a most terrible destructive storm, it commenced about ten and a half o'clock and continued some five hours and at four o'clock the morning of the 8th the entire garrison was flooded, by the middle of the day the water was 3 to 5 feet deep on the site of the fort, many of my employees and the enlisted men making narrow escapes with their lives and losing most of their clothing and other private property.
>
> Eight men were drowned, five of General Smith's orderlies, two of the 38th Infantry, and my principal herder Mr. Eli Watson (civilian) who lost his life while attempting to save the lives of several mules, he was an excellent and trusty man.
>
> Every effort was made, on the part of the quartermaster and employees to save the public property and they succeeded in saving the greater portion but all in a damaged condition.
>
> At about 12m. of the 8th I ordered my employees to construct boats with wagon boxes by putting paulins around them and by this means the entire garrison, by order of General A. J. Smith, commanding district of upper Arkansas, crossed to the east side of the north fork of Big Creek at 6 1/2 o'clock p. m. for safety and encamped on a high bluff for the night; 6 bodies of the drowned men had been recovered . . . and were buried near the post but not in a suitable manner, for want of lumber, being compelled to make the coffins from cracker boxes, etc.
>
> Since the water abated I have had all the packages of clothing and other property opened and the contents thoroughly dried and every means taken to prevent the stores from becoming a total loss.

Report on Indian Troubles on the Smoky Hill Trail, 1867

Indian resistance in the spring of 1867 inflicted heavy losses on the stage line operating along the Smoky Hill Trail. Lieutenant Colonel J.W. Davidson filed the following report after a special investigation of the situation on July 17, 1867:

> The facts acquired are substantially as follows. The United States Express Co. purchased from Wells Fargo Co. on the 1st February 1867, all their interest in the stage line carrying the United States mail from Junction City, Kansas to Denver City, Colorado, via the Smoky Hill route, paying for the same $292,087.92. The property consisted of 480 head of livestock (horses and mules), 19 concord coaches, 20 express

wagons, buggy division and blacksmith wagons, 40 stations including houses and barns all stocked for a daily line.

At this time the route from Lookout station to Willow Creek station was protected by guards of 10 to 15 soldiers at intermediate stations. During the month of February these guards were mostly withdrawn. There was no serious trouble with the Indians since the vacancy of the line, until the 15th of April last when they made a raid at Lookout station. From the conduct of the Indians however and hints thrown out by them, attacks all along the line were apprehended by the station keepers of the stage company to take place early in the summer.

Cut Nose and his band of about 20 in number were fed by the stage company from the 1st of February until about the 10th of April.

Appended to this marked "A" will be found an exhibit, showing the amount of losses inflicted by the Indian upon the U.S. Express Co. since the date above given, 15 April 1867. These losses total up: 134 horses, 41 mules, 440 tons of hay, 780 bushels corn, 605 bushels oats, 5 express wagons, 3 stations, 2 houses, 16 sets harness, 20 cords wood, 2 buggies, 2 cows, 1 passenger killed, 1 mail guard killed, 2 passengers wounded, 3 soldiers in coaches killed, 5 soldiers in coaches wounded, 5 employees of company killed.

The remainder of the report detailed how the army would attempt to protect what remained of the stage operation. Service would be cut from daily to triweekly runs of two coaches together. Four soldiers would ride as escorts on coaches east of Fort Hays; ten soldiers would serve as escorts west of Fort Hays. This plan, apparently followed as closely as possible, kept the stages running through most of the summer and fall of that year.

Illnesses Most Commonly Reported by Post Surgeon

Boils	Gun Shot Wounds
Bronchitis	Headache
Catarrh (influenza)	Hemorrhoids
Cholera	Inebriation
Colic	Laryngitis
Conjunctivitis	Neuralgia
Constipation	Rheumatism
Contusions	Sprains
Diarrhea	Syphilis
Fever	Tonsillitis
Frostbite	Ulcers
Gonorrhea	Wounds

Very few cases were reported of alcoholism, corns, delirium tremens, dropsy, earache, eczema, eye injury, fractures, heart disease, hernia, itch, jaundice, measles, pneumonia, ring worm, scabies, smallpox, sore throat, sunstroke, toothache, tumor, varicose veins, and whooping cough.

It must be noted that officers changed often, and some served many times. Commanding officers seldom served more than a few months at one time.

Captain Dewitt McMichael, Thirteenth Missouri Cavalry, 1865

Lieutenant Colonel William Tamblyn, First U.S. Volunteer Infantry, 1865–1866

First Lieutenant G.W.H. Stouch, Third Infantry, 1866–1867

Captain Albert P. Morrow, Seventh Cavalry, 1866–1867

Major Alfred Gibbs, Seventh Cavalry, 1867

Captain Henry Corbin, Thirty-eighth Infantry, 1867

Captain Samuel Ovenshine, Fifth Infantry, 1867–1871, 1876

*Major John E. Yard, Tenth Cavalry, 1868

Lieutenant Colonel Anderson D. Nelson, Fifth Infantry, 1868–1869

Colonel Nelson A. Miles, Fifth Infantry, 1869

Major George Gibson, Fifth Infantry, 1869–1871

Major Marcus H. Reno, Seventh Cavalry, 1870–1871

Colonel William B. Hazen, Sixth Infantry, 1871–1872

Major Robert M. Morris, Sixth Infantry, 1871–1872

Colonel Delancey Floyd Jones, Third Infantry, 1872–1873

First Lieutenant Joseph Hale, Third Infantry, 1872

Major Charles E. Compton, Sixth Cavalry, 1872–1873

Colonel James Oakes, Sixth Cavalry, 1873–1874

Captain Daniel Madden, Sixth Cavalry, 1874

Captain Charles H. Campbell, Sixth Cavalry, 1874–1875

Captain C.B. McLellan, Sixth Cavalry, 1875

First Lieutenant H.P. Perrine, Sixth Cavalry, 1875

Captain Julius W. Mason, Fifth Cavalry, 1875

Lieutenant Colonel Eugene A. Carr, Fifth Cavalry, 1875–1876

First Lieutenant Charles H. Rockwell, Fifth Cavalry, 1875

First Lieutenant Calbraith Rodgers, Fifth Cavalry, 1875

Captain Samuel S. Sumner, Fifth Cavalry, 1875–1876

First Lieutenant Richard Vance, Nineteenth Infantry, 1876–1877

Second Lieutenant George K. Spencer, Nineteenth Infantry, 1876

Captain Duncan M. Vance, Nineteenth Infantry, 1877–1878

First Lieutenant George M. Love, Sixteenth Infantry, 1878

Colonel Richard I. Dodge, Twenty-third Infantry, 1878–1879

First Lieutenant G. A. Goodale, Twenty-third Infantry, 1878

Captain James Henton, Twenty-third Infantry, 1878

First Lieutenant Charles Hay, Twenty-third Infantry, 1879

First Lieutenant Leopold O. Parker, Fourth Cavalry, 1879–1880

Major Henry E. Noyes, Fourth Cavalry, 1880

First Lieutenant Henry H. Bellas, Fourth Cavalry, 1880

Lieutenant Colonel Zenas R. Bliss, Nineteenth Infantry, 1880–1881

Captain John Lee, Fourth Cavalry, 1881

Captain Lloyd Wheaton, Twentieth Infantry, 1881–1882

Lieutenant Colonel N. A. M. Dudley, Ninth Cavalry, 1881–1885

Lieutenant Colonel C. Rodney Layton, Twentieth Infantry, 1883–1884

Captain John S. McNaught, Twentieth Infantry, 1883–1885

Captain Byron Dawson, Ninth Cavalry, 1884

First Lieutenant J.A. Manley, Twentieth Infantry, 1885

Second Lieutenant Benjamin Alvord, Twentieth Infantry, 1885

Lieutenant Colonel J. J. Coppinger, Eighteenth Infantry, 1885–1886

*Colonel John E. Yard, Eighteenth Infantry, 1886–1889

Captain George N. Bomford, Eighteenth Infantry, 1889

Captain William H. McLaughlin, Eighteenth Infantry, 1889

Major George K. Brady, Eighteenth Infantry, 1889

First Lieutenant Charles Hinton, Eighteenth Infantry, 1889

*Colonel Yard served at two ranks and with two different regiments. He was the only commanding officer to die in office.

Further Reading

Burkey, Blaine E. *Custer, Come at Once! The Fort Hays Years of George and Elizabeth Custer, 1867–1870.* Hays, Kans.: Thomas More Prep, 1976.

Custer, Elizabeth Bacon. *Following the Guidon.* Norman: University of Oklahoma Press, 1966.

Custer, Elizabeth Bacon. *Tenting on the Plains or, General Custer in Kansas and Texas.* Norman: University of Oklahoma Press, 1971.

Custer, George A. *My Life on the Plains or, Personal Experiences with Indians.* Norman: University of Oklahoma Press, 1962.

Leckie, William H. *The Buffalo Soldiers: A Narrative of the Negro Cavalry in the West.* Norman: University of Oklahoma Press, 1967.

Leckie, William H. *The Military Conquest of the Southern Plains.* Norman: University of Oklahoma Press, 1963.

Rickey, Don. *Forty Miles a Day on Beans and Hay: The Enlisted Soldier Fighting the Indian Wars.* Norman: University of Oklahoma Press, 1963.

Stallard, Patricia Y. *Glittering Misery: The Dependents of the Indian Fighting Army.* Fort Collins, Colo.: Old Army Press, 1978.

Utley, Robert M. *Frontier Regulars: The United States Army and the Indian, 1866–1891.* New York: Macmillan Publishing Co., 1973.

Utley, Robert M., ed. *Life in Custer's Cavalry: Diaries and Letters of Albert and Jennie Barnitz, 1867–1868.* New Haven: Yale University Press, 1977.

Acknowledgments

The author wishes to thank the following friends for help, information, and encouragement in the preparation of this material on Fort Hays: Jerry B. Ramsey, Timothy A. Zwink, Thomas C. Railsback, Reverend Blaine Burkey, Bob Wilhelm, Rodney Stabb, Ron Parks, and the late Raymond L. Welty. A special note of thanks is due my wife, Bonita, without whose assistance this never would have been completed.

Illustration Credits

This publication has been financed in part with federal funds from the National Park Service, a division of the United States Department of the Interior, and administered by the Kansas State Historical Society. The contents and opinions, however, do not necessarily reflect the views or policies of the United States Department of the Interior or the Kansas State Historical Society.